MY FIRST ENCYCLOPEDIA OF DINOSAURS

CLEVER
·Publishing·

CONTENTS

WHAT IS A DINOSAUR? 5

THE WORLD OF THE DINOSAURS 17

LARGE FAMILIES 31

LIFE OF THE DINOSAURS — 45

DINOSAUR PROFILES — 61

THE END OF THE DINOSAURS — 79

INDEX — 90

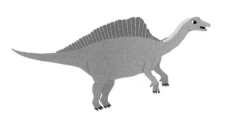

WHAT IS A DINOSAUR?

TERRIBLE LIZARDS

Like lizards, dinosaurs were land reptiles. In fact, their name means "terrible lizard." They first appeared on the planet a very long time ago and were the kings of the animal kingdom for many millions of years.

Lots of dinosaurs were gentle giants and fed on plants and leaves from trees. Animals that don't eat meat are called herbivores.

Others were fierce hunters with teeth as sharp as daggers, such as the famous *Tyrannosaurus rex*. Animals that eat meat are called carnivores.

Dinosaurs had a thick skin covered in scales. Some had plates and spikes that protected them from their enemies. Some even had feathers.

Some reptiles, like crocodiles, crawl on their bellies, with their legs out to the side. Having legs under their bodies made running quickly much easier for dinosaurs.

WHAT COLORS WERE DINOSAURS?

It's a mystery! To find out, we'd need to find pieces of skin, scales, or well-preserved feathers, which is incredibly difficult. But scientists continue to look for these.

Some dinosaurs were likely to have had very bright colors to scare their enemies.

Others were a similar shade to plants or trees, so they could hide among them.

To find a female mate, some males would have had very vibrant, lovely colors.

Dinosaurs With Four Feet

Dinosaurs with a long neck, armor, or a collar walked on four feet. Animals that walk on four feet are called quadrupeds.

Their feet were heavier than tree trunks in order to support their weight.

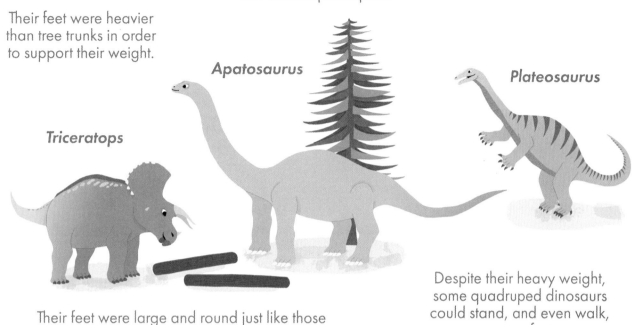

Apatosaurus

Plateosaurus

Triceratops

Their feet were large and round just like those of an elephant.

Despite their heavy weight, some quadruped dinosaurs could stand, and even walk, on two feet.

Dinosaurs With Two Feet

Many dinosaurs walked on their hind legs. Animals that walk on two feet are called bipeds.

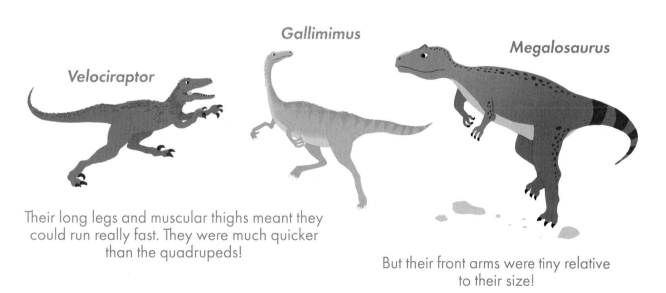

Gallimimus

Megalosaurus

Velociraptor

Their long legs and muscular thighs meant they could run really fast. They were much quicker than the quadrupeds!

But their front arms were tiny relative to their size!

FROM DWARVES TO GIANTS

Dinosaurs were the most gigantic animals ever seen on land. But while some were as big as buildings, others were as small as birds.

1. The smallest was the **Anchiornis**. This little guy was the size and weight of a pigeon.

11. **Lambeosauru**

10. **Brachiosaurus**

2. **Compsognathus**

3. **Velociraptor**

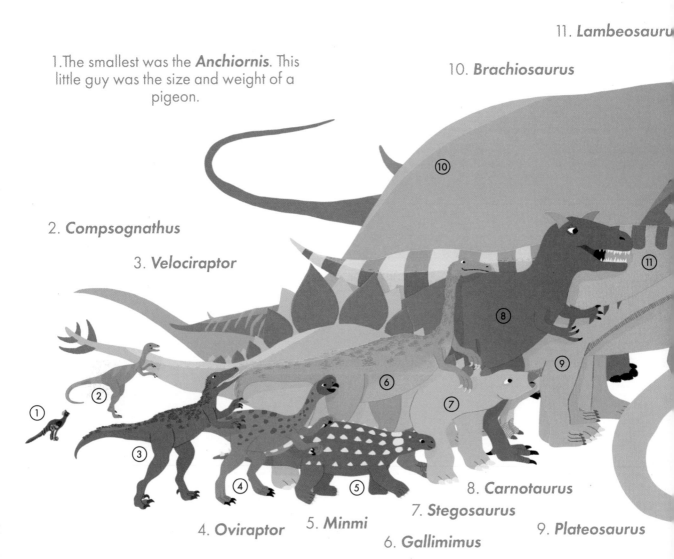

8. **Carnotaurus**

7. **Stegosaurus**

9. **Plateosaurus**

4. **Oviraptor**

5. **Minmi**

6. **Gallimimus**

12. The **Sauroposeidon** was the largest dinosaur. This giant was as high as a six-story building.

13. The **Seismosaurus** holds the record as the longest dinosaur. It was longer than three buses from head to tail.

17. **Diplodocus**

16. **Apatosaurus**

14. **Tyrannosaurus**

15. The biggest dinosaur footprint belongs to the **Argentinosaurus**. This colossal beast weighed as much as 15 African elephants.

UNBELIEVEABLE RECORDS

Dinosaurs were the strangest and most awesome animals that ever existed on our planet. They were also record-breaking reptiles.

The endless, whip-shaped tail of the **Diplodocus** measured 50 feet: that's as long as the width of a basketball court.

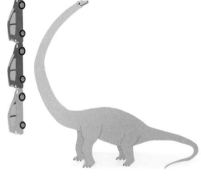

The **Mamenchisaurus** had the longest neck. It was over 40 feet (12 m), or about three cars.

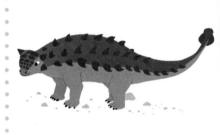

It was impossible for the **Ankylosaurus** to run fast with its heavy shell! It was one of the slowest dinosaurs.

Built like an ostrich, the **Struthiomimus** was capable of running 30 miles (50 km) per hour. If it was in danger, it could even reach 50 miles (80 km) per hour.

The **Therizinosaurus** had huge curved claws on its front feet. They were each as long as a person's arm.

The **Troodon** had the biggest brain of all the dinosaurs in relation to its size. It was the mos intelligent.

Unusual Records

Tarbosaurus had tiny arms for its size.

Torosaurus' head was the size of a car.

Mononykus had a single finger on each of its front feet.

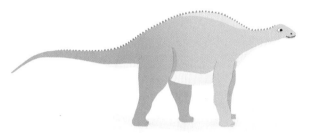

Brachytrachelopan had the shortest neck of the "long-necked" dinosaurs.

Stegosaurus had a brain as small as a nut.

Edmontosaurus' mouth had more than 1,000 teeth.

Look at the two pictures and spot the difference (5 things to find).
Spinosaurus had the highest dorsal fin, measuring up to 7 feet (2 m).

Have fun!

Answers: 1) Color of the tail stripes, 2) markings on back, 3) crest on head, 4) teeth, and 5) extra claw on back foot.

11

ALL SORTS OF HEADS

Dinosaurs had really weird heads. Some were plated, domed, or bumpy. Others featured horns, a beak, a crest, or a spiny collar!

Strange Collars

Styracosaurus:
spiky collar

Albertaceratops:
impressive design

Centrosaurus:
fierce horn

Einiosaurus:
nasal horn hook

Chasmosaurus:
giant shield

Regal Crests

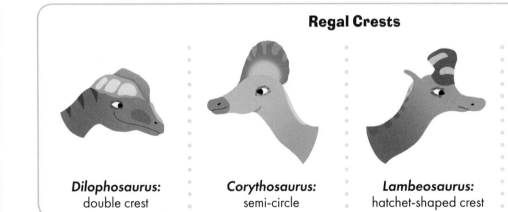

Dilophosaurus:
double crest

Corythosaurus:
semi-circle

Lambeosaurus:
hatchet-shaped crest

Parasaurolophus:
long, curved crest

Scary Heads

Pachycephalosaurus:
bony head covered in spikes

Stegoceras:
bony head covered in bump

Goyocephale:
completely encased
helmet-head

Horned Heads

Carnotaurus:
bull-like horns

Tsintaosaurus:
unicorn-like horn

Stygimoloch:
demon-like head

Beak Shapes

Psittacosaurus:
parrot-like beak

Anatotitan:
duck-like beak

Dromiceiomimus:
ostrich-like beak

INCREDIBLE TO LOOK AT

An incredible variety of dinosaurs roamed the earth. Some of these "terrible lizards" were terrifying to behold. Which one looks the fiercest to you?

Suchomimus had the head of a crocodile on the body of a **Tyrannosaurus**.

Silvisaurus had sides that were covered with fearsome spikes.

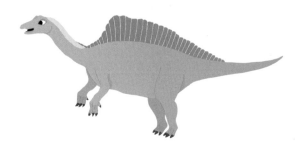

Ouranosaurus had a dorsal sail (spine) supported by long, bony quills.

Irritator had a crocodile mouth, dorsal sail, and a crest!

Kentrosaurus had a double row of plates and very scary spikes!

Amargasaurus had a really strange, thorny crest and long neck and back.

Despite its bulky body shape, its huge collar, and its ferocious look, the **Achelousaurus** was a peaceful plant eater.

With its armored body, bony nails, its hammer tail, and its pointed horns, the **Euoplocephalus** was a walking fortress.

With its heavy vertical spikes and bony nails on its back and tail, the **Polacanthus** looked a little like a cactus.

The **Giganotosaurus** was even bigger than a **Tyrannosaurus**! Its enormous jaws were filled with teeth up to 8 inches (20 cm) long.

Find the right shadow for this Huayangosaurus.
Discovered in China, the **Huayangosaurus** was smaller than its cousin, the **Stegosaurus**.

1.   **2.**   **3.**

Have fun!

Answer: Shadow number 2

THE WORLD OF THE DINOSAURS

THE FIRST DINOSAURS

The history of planet Earth is divided into several different time periods. Dinosaurs first appeared at the end of the Triassic period. This period was a long time ago and the world was very different than it is now.

The Earth was made up of one massive continent in the middle of a vast ocean.

In forests, huge ferns and giant conifer trees grew. There were also vast deserts.

Giant dragonflies, enormous spiders, and huge centipedes lived in the forests.

Dinosaurs were not yet rulers of the natural world. Other ancient reptiles occupied the land, seas, rivers, and even the sky!

The first mammals were very small and looked a bit like mice with long, pointed snouts.

Huge frogs and enormous turtle lived in streams, while flying lizards roamed the sky.

Meet some Triassic dinosaurs:

Plateosaurus was as long as a bus!

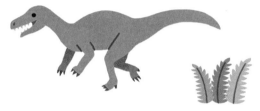

Eoraptor is one of the oldest known dinosaurs.

Staurikosaurus had sharp, pointed teeth.

Herrerasaurus was a fierce hunter with long, curved claws.

Procompsognathus used its speed and agility to leap on its prey.

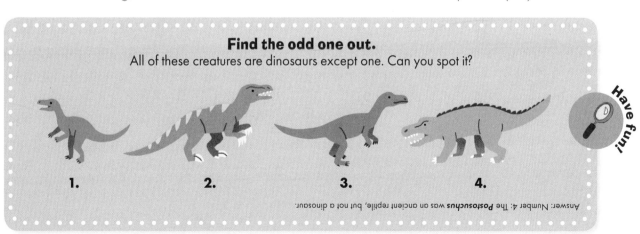

Find the odd one out.
All of these creatures are dinosaurs except one. Can you spot it?

1.   **2.**   **3.**   **4.**

Have fun!

Answer: Number 4: The **Postosuchus** was an ancient reptile, but not a dinosaur.

19

THE TIME OF WALKING GIANTS

The Triassic period was followed by the Jurassic, when dinosaurs became the rulers of Earth. It was then that the biggest animals on the planet emerged, known as the "long necks."

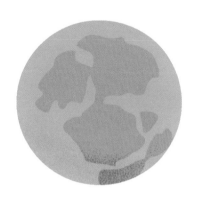

Very, very slowly, the single continent broke into two pieces and, during the Jurassic, those two pieces began to separate.

It was hot and rained a lot. The deserts became swamps and wetlands. The Earth was covered in forests.

Pine trees and other evergreens and conifers grew taller and taller. So did ferns.

The plant-eating dinosaurs (herbivores) became giants. To hunt them, carnivores (meat eaters) had to become more and more ferocious.

On the ground, lizards and small mammals lived alongside dinosaurs. Also, the first birds appeared.

In the air the flying reptiles were charge. In the ocean giant reptil attacked anything that swam.

Meet some Jurrasic dinosaurs:

Apatosaurus had a long whip-like tail.

Megalosaurus was one of the first dinosaurs ever discovered.

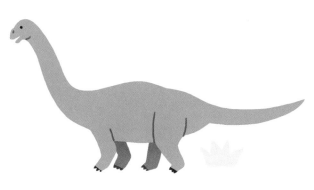

Allosaurus was even bigger and more terrifying than **Megalosaurus**.

Camarasaurus, a herbivore, was hunted by meat-eaters like **Allosaurus**.

Lesothosaurus was a herbivore that looked like a hunter.

Barosaurus was closely related to the **Diplodocus**.

FLOWERS AND BEASTS

The Jurrasic period was followed by the Cretaceous period. It was during this period that dinosaurs with horns, armor, and collars started to appear--and the first flowers bloomed.

The continents continued to separate from each other, creating vast oceans between them. The climate also cooled a little.

Forests of leafy trees such as oak trees formed. Conifers continued to grow, too.

The first flowers appeared: magnolias, roses, and primroses Lilies (lily pads) floated on the surface of lakes.

In the sea, there were many fish of all shapes and sizes. Some swam in big groups called schools.

Small mammals, such as *Zalambdalestes*, remained hidden to avoid being eaten by carnivores.

A number of flying species of birds appeared. They shared the sky with huge flying reptiles.

Meet some Cretaceous dinosaurs:

Protoceratops was one of the first "horned dinosaurs"--but its horn wasn't fully developed.

Alamosaurus was one of the last long-necked dinosaurs.

Gorgosaurus means "ferocious lizard".

Pinacosaurus used its clubbed tail as a deadly weapon.

Caudipteryx was covered in feathers.

Prenocephale had a bony head, as hard as a helmet.

Which Cretaceous dinosaur made each shadow?

1.

2.

3.

4.

Have fun!

Answers: 1. Protoceratops 2. Pinacosaurus 3. Prenocephale 4. Caudipteryx.

23

KINGS OF THE SKY

During the same era as the dinosaurs, strange feathered creatures with wings flew in the sky: **Pterosaurs**. They preceded the first birds, and their name means "winged lizard."

Eudimorphodon flew by beating its wings.

Pteranodon glided, carried by the wind.

Quetzalcoatl was the size of a small plane.

You can recognize **Tapejara** by its dome-shaped crest.

The long tail of **Peteinosaurus** acted as a rudder.

Perched or on the ground, **Batrachognathus** used its wings to balance.

Pterodaustro fed by filtering the water, like a flamingo.

WHAT'S ON THE MENU?

Rhamphorhynchus ate fish.

Dimorphodon ate insects and lizards.

Anurognathus ate flying insects.

Dsungaripterus ate seafood.

What was the favorite meal of an *Ichthyornis*? Fish.

With its incredibly tiny wings, it was impossible for the *Hesperornis* to fly.

Baptornis couldn't fly, but it swam and it dove very well.

Forest Birds

Yixianornis flew skillfully between the trees.

Sinornis flew very well and also climbed trees.

Iberomesornis hunted insects.

Confuciusornis was very good at climbing and flying!

BIZARRE BIRD

The **Archaeopteryx** was one of the first birds. It had wings, feathers, and a beak like modern birds. But it also had teeth, claws on its wings, and a long bony tail like a reptile!

Did you know?

TERRORS OF THE RIVERS AND OCEANS

If the dinosaurs were the kings of the land, marine reptiles were the princes of the oceans. These monsters terrorized everything that lived in the sea. In rivers, the giant crocodiles were just as terrifying!

Elasmosaurus didn't swim fast, but thanks to its super-long neck, it could catch fish in a flash!

Mosasaurus was a formidable hunter. Its jaws were lined with razor-sharp, hooked teeth.

The massive **Kronosaurus** had a head over 10 feet (3 m) long and huge, dagger-like teeth.

Ichthyosaurus was a fast swimmer. This reptile resembled a dolphin and ate fish, octopus, and cuttlefish.

Liopleurodon was one of the greatest carnivores of the sea. Its favorite prey? **Ichthyosaurs**. Yummy!

Nothosaurus mostly lived in water, but also liked to rest on the beach--like a modern-day seal.

Meet more aquatic beasts:

Leedsichthys was a fish as big as a whale.

Hybodus, a shark, was tasty prey for *Liopleurodon*.

Henodus was a marine reptile that resembled a flattened tortoise.

Psephoderma was a bizarre-looking, seafood-eating reptile.

Archelon was the biggest marine turtle that ever existed.

Teleosaurus was a marine crocodile that ate fish and squid.

SUPER-CROC ATTACKS

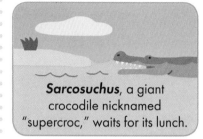

Sarcosuchus, a giant crocodile nicknamed "supercroc," waits for its lunch.

An *Ouranosaurus* arrives at the riverside.

Supercroc leaps out of the water like a monster!

It snaps its enormous jaws around the dinosaur

... and drags it to the bottom of the river.

LAND NEIGHBORS

On land, dinosaurs lived among a variety of animals: from tiny to large, from gentle to dangerous. Some were strange to behold--others were terrifying.

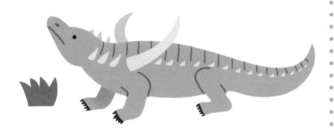

Despite its menacing appearance, **Desmatosuchus** was a peaceful herbivore. Its two long horns protected it from its enemies.

This animal is called a **Hyperodapedon**. With its powerful beak and teeth, it could eat the hardest grains of ferns and other plants.

The **Placerias** looked like a hippopotamus. It dug up plant roots for food, and was strong enough to defend itself from enemies.

The **Massetognathus'** body, hairy tail, and narrow muzzle made it look like a mammal, but it was a reptile.

The Boar Crocodile

Did you know?

Unlike the majority of crocodiles, the **Kaprosuchus** lived on land. It was a ferocious killer that could move fast. Its teeth resembled boar tusks, which is why it was called the boar crocodile.

The Tiniest Ones

All these small mammals appeared during the age of the dinosaurs. Look closely at them. They look a lot like animals you see today.

Shrew

Squirrel

Megazostrodon: It's a shrew lookalike!

Crusafontia: It looks like a squirrel!

Opossum

Pyrenean desman

Flying squirrel

Alphadon: It's the spitting image of an opossum!

Zalambdalestes: It resembles the Pyrenean desman family.

Volaticotherium: This guy is a copy of the flying squirrel!

A Tiny "Giant"

Although the **Didelphodon** only weighed a few pounds, it was one of the largest mammals of its time--and, therefore, one of the biggest mammals the dinosaurs ever encountered.

Did you know?

LARGE FAMILIES

· ·

THE LONG NECKS

The long-neck dinosaurs were so called for their super-long necks connected to small heads. Their bodies were huge, with very long tails. They were the tallest, longest, and heaviest of the dinosaurs.

Their huge necks allowed them to tear leaves off the tops of trees, much like modern-day giraffes.

Their rake-like teeth were very useful for pulling leaves from branches.

These giants spent their days swallowing thousands of leaves.

Their long, powerful tails could be used as a whip if attacked.

The long necks lived in herds, which made it easier to defend against predators.

The **Supersaurus** was one of the giants of the long necks. It was bigger than the **Diplodocus** but not as big as the **Seismosaurus**.

The **Brachiosaurus** was as tall as a five-story building. Reaching for tasty leaves from the highest branches was no trouble at all.

The **Camarasaurus** had large, tightly packed teeth shaped like spoons. No plant could escape its solid dentures!

The **Alamosaurus** used its long tail like a crutch to support itself when it stood up on its back legs.

The Armored Long Necks!

Saltasaurus and *Agustinia* were strange, even for long necks. The first had a back covered in bony plates with horned edges and bumps. The second had a spiny crest from its head down to its tail--not a very appetizing treat for a carnivore!

Saltasaurus

Agustinia

Did you know?

33

(See portrait of a *Diplodocus* on pages 66–67)

THICK HEADS AND DUCK BEAKS

During the Cretaceous period, there were dinosaurs with thick skulls that were either curved or flat. These were called "thick head lizards." This was also the era of the "duck beaks": dinosaurs with large beak-like mouths and sometimes even funny crests.

The biggest of the thick heads was **Pachycephalosaurus**. It was as long as a truck and taller than an elephant.

The tiniest of this group was the **Stegoceras**. It was smaller than a person, but it didn't hesitate to charge at its enemies with its helmet head.

During mating season, the male **Homalocephale** fought head to head with its rivals. The winner became the chief of the group, which included the females.

The **Tylocephale** holds the record for the thickest skull. Its name means "swollen head".

The **Stygimoloch** is the only type in this group to have large horns around its thick skull and spikes along its muzzle.

The **Prenocephale**'s enormous, egg-shaped dome was made of a thick, hard bone that protected its brain during fights.

The Duck Beaks

The duck beaks had neither horns nor spikes or sharp claws to defend themselves.

When in danger there were two types of defense:
To **run** ...

... or **dive** into the water and **swim** away!

They lived **in herds** and ate together. They ate stems, roots, and leaves.
They cut their food with the sharp edges of their **beaks**.

Each species had a different type of crest, which is a good way to identify each one.

To communicate, they **bellowed**.

(See the picture of a **Parasaurolophus** on pages 70–71.)

THE BREAST PLATES

In order to protect themselves, these armored dinosaurs had an array of weapons: thorns and spikes, plates and bony nails, hammer tails or spiked tails. These were all very off-putting to hungry carnivores looking for something to eat!

A bony outer shell protected them from the neck to the tail. They were like walking tanks!

This type of dinosaur walked on **four legs** and ate ferns and other plants.

The **Nodosaurus** and its young had less armor and no hammer tail.

Ankylosaurus and its relations had big hammers at the end of their tails.

 **Strange Armor!**

The **Stegosaurus** and its cousins had huge bony plates and spikes along their back and tail. Some of these spikes measured over 3 feet (1 m) long!

(See the **Stegosaurus** picture on pages 76–77.)

(See a picture of the **Ankylosaurus** on pages 74–75.)

The *Ankylosaurus* family: Armored reptiles

Saichania: Its body was covered in triangular spikes.

Talarurus: Its tail could break the bones of its enemies!

The *Nodosaurus* Family: The Bumpy Reptiles

Edmontonia: Its armor was embellished with nails and spikes.

Polacanthus: Its spines were its weapons.

The *Stegosaurus* Family: the Roof Lizards

Dacentrurus: It had very sharp spikes, especially on its tail.

Lexovisaurus: It had terrifyingly long spikes on each of its shoulders.

THE HORNED COLLARS

Some quadruped dinosaurs were well known for their strange collars and their long horns. They belonged to the "horned faces" family. The most famous of this group? Triceratops of course!

Like other members of its family, the collar of the **Brachyceratops** was made of skin-covered bones.

With its powerful parrot-like beak, the **Protoceratops** could rip and tear even the toughest leaves.

Pachyrhinosaurus ddidn't hav a horn; it had something like a bony ball on its nose. Was it use to beat its rivals? That remains a mystery.

To scare its enemies, **Diabloceratops** lowered its head, raised and shook its collar, and charged with its horns forward.

Collars could also be used to help find a female mate. **Pentaceratops** proudly showed off its collar in front of females.

The collar protected the neck of the horned faces. With its collar, **Torosaurus** had nothing to fear.

A DAY IN THE LIFE OF A STYRACOSAURUS

A male and female **Styracosaurus** graze side by side.

Attracted by the pretty female, another male approaches.

The two male rivals face each other, their collars on full view.

Whichever is the most impressive will stay with the female.

The dinosaur who lost the fight will have to leave in search for **another female**.

Suddenly, a **Daspletosaurus** appears behind them!

The **Styracosaurus** just has time to turn around ...

... and plant his enormous horn in the **Daspletosaurus's** stomach.

He might not have found his mate today, but he did save his own life!

39

(See pages 74–75 for more details on **Triceratops**.)

REPTILE BULLIES AND THEIR GANG

These large two-legged (biped) carnivores were terrifying creatures. Some were real monsters! The smaller carnivores were less striking, but they were just as frightening. All of them were ferocious hunters.

The Little Bullies

Compsognathus had fine, razor-sharp teeth.

Dilong, cousin of the fierce-looking **Tyrannosaurus**, had a fluffy tail.

Troodon could hunt equally as well by day or by night.

Noasaurus was so lightweight that it could easily pounce on its prey.

Coelophysis had little, finger-like claws that were perfect for catching tiny beasts.

BEWARE OF THE FEATHERED DINOSAURS!

A group of small carnivorous dinosaurs, named "running reptiles," had feathers over their bodies. Fast and cunning, they hunted in packs. Here are three of these merciless hunters:

Velociraptor

Dromaeosaurus

Deinonychus

(See pages 62–63 for a picture of the *Tyrannosaurus*.)

The Giants

Tyrannosaurus is the most famous of the "tyrant reptiles".

Tyrannotitan a name that means "giant tyrant,"--was a real terror!

Cryolophosaurus had an interesting crest.

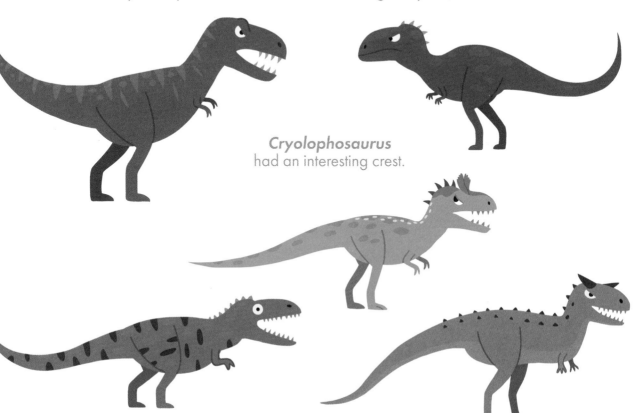

Carcharodontosaurus had teeth like those of an enormous shark.

Carnotaurus was one of the meanest hunters in the world of dinosaurs.

The Profile of a Killer

The **Utahraptor** was one of the most dangerous killers in the dinosaur world. It had several fierce features that it used to hunt and defend itself.

A scythe-like claw on each foot

Hands with three claws that cut like knives

A powerful jaw with sharp teeth like a saw.

Did you know?

THE OSTRICH DINOSAURS

The members of this group of dinosaurs were called "bird impersonators" and closely resembled ostriches. That's why they are often called ostrich dinosaurs.

Their toothless beaks were just like a bird's beak.

They had long legs. The **Struthiomimus** had very muscular ones.

Like the duck beak family, the ostrich dinosaurs didn't have any means of defense ... but they could run fast! **Dromiceiomimus** could run as fast as 40 miles (65 km) per hour for short distances.

To keep safe, the ostrich dinosaurs moved together in herds. Their long, stiff tails helped them keep their balance when running.

The biggest of this group was the **Gallimimus**.

LUNCH WITH THE ORNITHOMIMUS

A group of **Ornithomimus** have just woken up. They're hungry.

Not a problem; they eat both plants and animals.

One of them spots some delicious, juicy berries.

Using its fingers, it grabs the branch to its beak and feasts.

Its friends prefer to grab plump and tender flying insects.

Another catches a small lizard that didn't run away fast enough. What a morning treat!

Over 200 Teeth!

Pelecanimimus is the oldest known ostrich dinosaur. Unlike its younger cousins, its beak was lined with 220 tiny, pointed teeth.

Did you know?

LIFE OF THE DINOSAURS

NESTS AND EGGS

Like all reptile mothers, dinosaur mothers laid eggs. Some brooded (sat on their eggs), some didn't. When they were ready to hatch, baby dinosaurs broke the shell of their eggs with a tiny fang on the top of their muzzle, just like little chicks!

Plant-eating dinosaurs (herbivores) built their nests next to one another. That way, they could all be better protected from egg eaters.

Many dinosaurs dug a hole in the ground. The **Protoceratops** mommy preferred to build her nest in the sand.

The bigger dinosaurs, such as the **Apatosaurus**, could not sit on their eggs. The shells would break under their weight.

Much smaller dinosaurs, such as **Oviraptors**, could sit on their eggs without breaking them. They were also protecting them from egg hunters.

The Story of Eggs

Dinosaur eggs had a hard shell. The smallest ones were the same size as chicken eggs. The biggest were 3 to 4 times bigger than ostrich eggs ... which is still very small compared to the size of the dinosaurs that laid them!

Velociraptor
egg

Protoceratops
egg

Hypselosaurus
egg

Hadrosaurus
egg

A baby dinosaur
inside its egg

THE NEST OF THE MAIASAURA, THE "GOOD MOM"

The *Maiasaura* mom builds her nest on a hill shielded from floods.

She digs a big hole in the ground in the shape of a **basin** ...

... and covers up the bottom with **ferns**.

Then she lays her **eggs** there and covers them up ...

... with a big bunch of **leaves** to keep them warm.

She rests next to the nest, ready to defend it from egg **thieves**!

The eggs are **hatching**! The *Maiasaura* mom frees the nest from the leaves ...

... in order to help the babies to get out. They are so cute!

A DINOSAUR CHILDHOOD

Many dinosaurs looked after their young ones. They brought them food and protected them from predators. However, not all newborns were this lucky, and some had to look after themselves from the minute they were born!

The **Maiasaura** were good parents. In fact, their name means "good mother lizard."

They could have 30 young ones at once. They certainly had big families!

While daddy dinosaur guarded the nest ...

... mommy dinosaur went to fetch food for her babies.

She brought them leaves and seeds.

As they grew bigger, the young ones left the nest ...

... but never went too far away from their mommy.

RESOURCEFUL BABIES

As soon as their eggs hatch, **Orodromeus** dinosaur babies leave their nest.

Their parents are not around to protect or feed them.

Carefree, they roam around in search of food.

Just what this **Troodon** was looking for ... on the hunt for helpless babies.

Could the **Troodon** quickly catch one between its clawed fingers?

Suddenly panicking, the baby dinosaurs run away in all directions.

Look at the two pictures and spot the difference (5 things to find).

Hypacrosaurus were also very good parents.

Have fun!

Answer: 1) Bigger crest on the male dinosaur, 2) a bit of eggshell on the head of one baby, 3) open mouth of the female dinosaur, 4) leaf color 5) and one dinosaur baby has its feet outside the nest.

ON THE ROAD

Large herds of plant-eating dinosaurs often traveled far in order to hunt for food or to escape the cold winters. The journeys were often filled with many dangers along the way.

Alamosauruses traveled towards new forests to eat.

Many carnivores would follow them ready to charge at a lost young one or a sick, weak adult.

Crossing rivers could be very dangerous

The **Deinosuchus**, otherwise known as the "terrible crocodile," would wait around the river patiently for long necks or horned heads to cross the river.

STRENGTH IN UNITY

A **Chasmosaurus** herd is quietly eating.

A couple of **Daspletosauruses** come closer.

They would very much like two young dinosaurs for lunch.

The adults have noticed the danger. They gather their young ones at the center of the herd.

Then they form a circle around them ...

... with their heads down, their collars on full view, and horns facing forward.

Faced with all those pointy horns, the **Daspletosauruses** decide to give up their attack.

Finally, the danger is out of sight ...

... and the **Chasmosauruses** can go back to eating their tasty fern meal.

DINNER IS READY

Most dinosaurs were herbivores, which means their meals were mostly leaves. Some were meat eaters, and others were omnivores – which means that they ate everything.

Plant Eaters

No need to argue about food. Everyone ate whatever they could reach.

With shorter necks, **Brachytrachelopans** ate leaves off low branches.

The **Pelorosaurus** had a feast with the leaves they found at the tops of the highest trees.

Minmi grazed on low-lying fern and bushes.

Up on their hind legs, the tiny **Microceratus** nibbled on the leaves of Cycas trees.

With their beaks, the **Ouranosaurus** pulled plants out from wet ground.

Did you know?

There was a plant eater full of sharp teeth.
The **Heterodontosaurus**, also known as the "different toothed lizard," had three different types of teeth.

1. Pointy and coned-shaped teeth for cutting.

2. Two long, curved fangs for piercing food.

3. Large, chisel-like teeth for grinding.

Omnivores

Pelecanimimus ate plants and tiny fish.

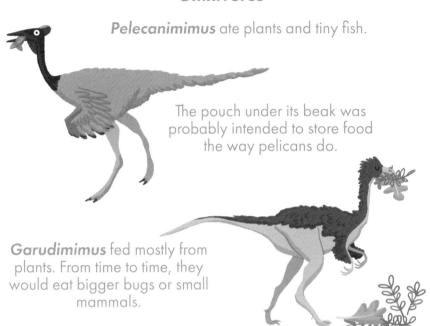

The pouch under its beak was probably intended to store food the way pelicans do.

Garudimimus fed mostly from plants. From time to time, they would eat bigger bugs or small mammals.

For a *Harpymimus*, a meal consisted of plants, insects, lizards, and other small animals.

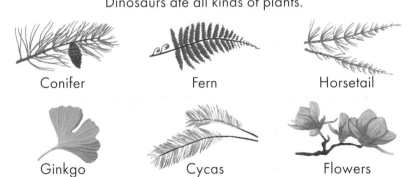

DINOSAURS' FAVORITE PLANTS
Dinosaurs ate all kinds of plants.

Conifer

Fern

Horsetail

Ginkgo

Cycas

Flowers

STONES IN THE STOMACH!

Psittacosaurus cut the leaves and hard stems off the trees ...

... and ate them without chewing.

To help them digest they would swallow stones.

When rolling around in their stomach, these stones would help crush their meal into mush.

SKILLED HUNTERS

Carnivores had different methods for hunting. Some preferred to hunt alone. Others hunted in groups in order to circle around their prey. Some attacked by surprise and others ran after their prey.

Ceratosaurus hunted on their own or in pairs. Their favorite prey consisted of small dinosaurs such as the **Dryosaurus** pictured here.

Ornitholestes had their own favorite meal: lizards. They caught them with their arms and crushed them in a single bite!

Strong and fast, the **Albertosaurus** ran after plant-eating dinosaurs or leapt at them while they were eating.

The **Harpymimus** were very good runners. They were fast enough to catch flying insects and capture lizards.

When hunting, a **Tarbosaurus** would lie in wait, hidden behind trees. Having spotted its prey, the beast would attack with its mouth wide open.

The very quick and ferocious **Velociraptors** had a lethal weapon: a strong claw on each foot, which they used as daggers.

A GROUP ATTACK BY DEINONYCHUSES

A *Tenontosaurus* has left its herd in order to get some water.

That is precisely what a group of *Deinonychus* has been waiting for ...

... a lonely dinosaur to attack.

They leap at the unlucky plant eater ...

... and bite into it from all sides.

Alone and facing a group of starving predators, the *Tenontosaurus* has no chance to escape.

Fatally wounded, it collapses ...

... and the *Deinonychuses* can start feasting.

SPECIAL MEALS

Some carnivores had special tastes and specific meals. Some only fed on insects or fish. Others just ate dead animals. Some even ate each other—scary!

The **Baryonyx** grabbed fish with its giant claws or caught them with its muscular crocodile jaw.

With its long teeth, the **Suchomimus** could catch huge slippery fish and gobble them all in one go.

The always hungry **Carcharodontosaurus** would often eat the remains of other dead dinosaurs—gross!

A mighty carnivore, the **Majungasaurus** was also a cannibal: it would even eat others from its own species.

Did you know?

Wrongly accused!
For a long time, the **Coelophysis** was thought to devour its own babies. A recent study showed that the small skeleton found in the stomach of an adult **Coelophysis** wasn't a baby of its own, but, instead, a small crocodile.

Bug Eaters

Microraptor hunted insects among the trees.

Procompsognathus had pointy teeth that could pierce through the tough shell of beetles.

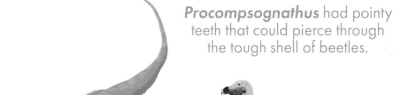

Saltopus was particularly fond of crunching cockroaches.

Avimimus could be found running at full speed to catch flying bugs.

Coelophysis could catch giant dragonflies.

Who eats what?
Match each dinosaur with its favorite meal!

1. *Baryonyx* **2.** *Coelophysis* **3.** *Carcharodontosaurus* **4.** *Ornitholestes* **5.** *Saltopus*

A **B** **C** **D** **E**

Have fun!

Answers: 1C, 2E, 3B, 4A, 5D

HERBIVORES VS. CARNIVORES

When a carnivore attacked a shelled dinosaur, or a horned or long-neck dinosaur, the winner wasn't necessarily the meat eater. Plant eaters were well equipped to win fights and save their own lives.

Brontomerus's strong kick can hurt the smaller *Deinonychus*.

Giganotosaurus must beware of *Argentinosaurus's* mighty tail.

Triceratops can pierce *Tyrannosaurus* with its horns.

Kentrosaurus's spikes can defeat *Ceratosaurus*.

Albertosaurus may lose to *Ankylosaurus's* clubbed tail.

Therizinosaurus's scythe-like claws can cut **Tarbosaurus** down.

Gastonia's spikey, armored shell protects it from **Utahraptor**.

Iguanodon's spur-shaped thumbs can defeat **Acrocanthosaurus**.

DEFENSE TACTIC FROM THE HYLAE-SAURUS

When threatened, **Hylaesaurus** crouched down ...

... folding its legs under its body and clawing the ground below.

Firmly rooted to the ground, it stayed motionless.

Its bony, nail-dotted armor covered with spikes prevented attackers from harming it. How crafty!

DINOSAUR PROFILES

TYRANNOSAURUS REX

Tyrannosaurus rex, also known as ***T-rex***, is the most famous of the big, bad dinosaurs. Its apt name means "king of the tyrant reptiles". It was a giant beast that terrorized other dinosaurs.

The ***T-rex*** was as long as a bus, as tall as a giraffe and as heavy as an elephant. It lived towards the end of the Cretaceous era in North America.

Its sharp teeth measured as long as 20 cm (7.8 inches).

A meat-eater, it also fed from dead animals. After all, it it required less effort than hunting!

ITS HUNTING MODE: LIE IN WAIT

The **Tyrannosaurus rex** is hiding behind the trees, amid the gigantic fern ...

... in order to attack its prey by surprise.

Like a devil, it suddenly appears and leaps at the **Anatotitan** ...

... and sinks its teeth into its body!

With his mighty jaw, it pulls out a big chunk of flesh ...

... and, just like a crocodile, swallows it whole without chewing it!

Tiny little arms
T-rex's arms were so small that it couldn't reach its own mouth. It had two thin, sharp, claw-like fingers at the end of each arm.

Did you know?

SPINOSAURUS

Spinosaurus means "spine lizard". How fitting! Along the back of this most peculiar looking dinosaur ran a long row of spines, some of them taller than a human being!

Spinosaurus lived in the middle of the Cretaceous era in North Africa.

Its spines were covered by skin, making it look like a sail on its back!

When it ran, it used its long tail to keep its balance.

It ate many different animals. Its favorite were large fish.

Its jaws were filled with many pointy teeth, very useful for catching fish!

WHAT DID IT USE ITS BIG SAIL FOR?

How spinosaurus used its sail still remains a mystery ...

Perhaps the **Spinosaurus**'s sail helped the dinosaur stay warm by absorbing sunlight ...

... and when it was too hot, it could **cool down** by exposing it to the cool winds.

Its sail might have been used to **intimidate predators**, making it appear larger than it was ...

... or, perhaps it was used to **attract** females during mating season. It would have had to be very colorful in order to attract a mate.

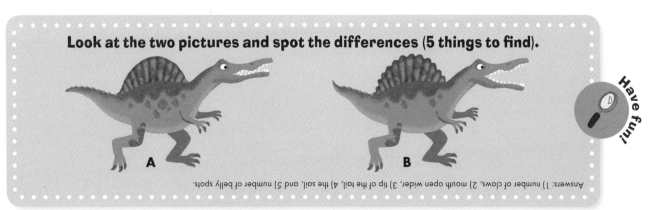

Look at the two pictures and spot the differences (5 things to find).

A

B

Have fun!

Answers: 1) number of claws, 2) mouth open wider, 3) tip of the tail, 4) the sail, and 5) number of belly spots.

DIPLODOCUS

The most famous of the long necks is the **Diplodocus**. This giant dinosaur was longer than a tennis court, as heavy as 2 or 3 elephants and as tall as a giraffe ... and of course it had a its gigantic neck.

Diplodocus means 'double beam': its name comes from the shape of some of the bones along its long tail.

It lived at the end of the Jurassic period in North America.

Its neck measured over 7 meters, which is roughly the height of a house!

Although it was very heavy, it could raise itself up using its tail

It could also swim.

Its tail was twice as long as its neck!

It always ate and traveled in a herd.

The **Diplodocus** used its tail to whip or hit its enemies. An **Allosaurus** would have had to think twice about attacking it.

The tip of its tail was thin like a whip. When it waved and cracked it, it produced a deafening, gunshot noise which scared its attackers away!

Its long, thin teeth looked like little pencils. It could also grow brand new teeth when it needed to.

TEETH LIKE A RAKE

To get food, the **Diplodocus** reached out and grabbed the branch of a tree with its mouth.

With its pointy teeth positioned along the start of its jaw like a rake...

... it could pull out the leaves and buds from the branch by tilting back of its head.

IGUANODON

Iguanodon was one of the very first dinosaurs ever discovered. Its teeth looked like an iguana's; that's why its name literally means "iguana teeth". *Iguanodons* were very common and lived all over the world.

Iguanodon lived in herds at the start of the Cretaceous period.

Its favourite plants were fern, conifer and ginkgo.

It walked slowly on four legs ...

... but when in danger, it could flee very fast on its hind legs!

A tall plant-eater, it would chew on its food a long time before swallowing it ...

... and to help digestion, it would eat rocks!

Friends of the Iguanodon

Silvisaurus had mighty spikes, but no lethal thumb.

Sauropelta had an armored back and fierce spikes.

Tenontosaurus walked just as well on two legs as it did on four.

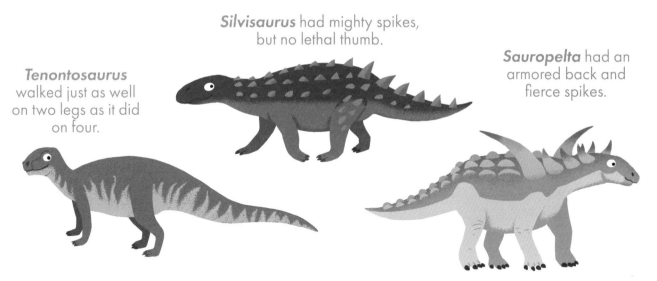

Enemies of the Iguanodon

Acrocanthosaurus terrorized *Iguanodons*.

Deinonychus would attack in groups.

Utahraptor was one of *Iguanodons*'s worst nightmares!

Lethal thumbs

Two of *Iguanodon*'s thumbs were shaped like sharp spikes. It could easily stab an enemy in the neck or burst its eyes.

Did you know?

69

PARASAUROLOPHUS

With its funny crest in the shape of a tube, it would have been impossible to confuse **Parasaurolophus** with another dinosaur. Its crest helped to carry the sound of its cry far away. It wasn't one for keeping quiet!

Parasaurolophus could be found in North America towards the end of the Cretaceous period.

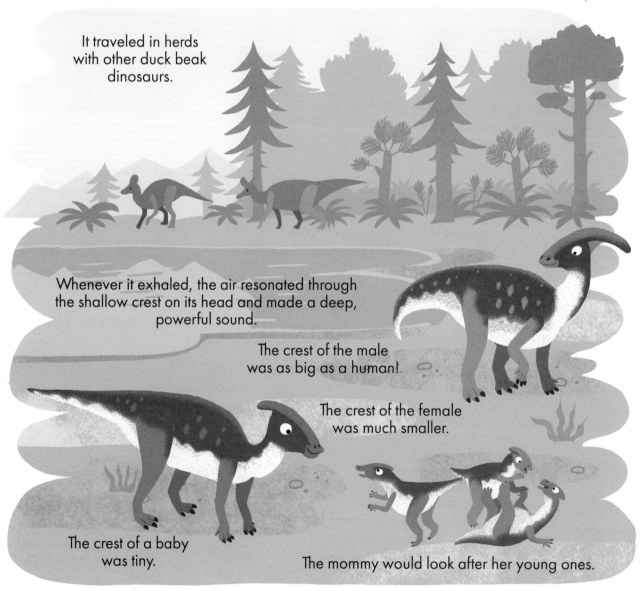

It traveled in herds with other duck beak dinosaurs.

Whenever it exhaled, the air resonated through the shallow crest on its head and made a deep, powerful sound.

The crest of the male was as big as a human!

The crest of the female was much smaller.

The crest of a baby was tiny.

The mommy would look after her young ones.

RUN AWAY NOW!

It's time to eat. The **Parasaurolophus** are hungry.

From afar, a **Tyrannosaurus rex** creeps closer.

But it's been spotted by a male from the herd ...

... which immediately lets out a huge cry to signal danger to the others.

Scared, the tall plant-eaters quickly run away ...

... with the hungry **T-rex** close behind!

Some of them jump in the water and swim away ....

... using their tail as a paddle to go faster.

TRICERATOPS

Triceratops is probably as famous as its biggest enemy, the **T-rex**. It looked like a much bigger and stronger version of a rhinoceros. It certainly wasn't afraid to stand up to the "king of the tyrant lizards".

Triceratops means "head with three horns".

Triceratops is one of the last dinosaurs from the Cretaceous period. They lived in herds in the valleys of North America.

How long were its horns? Over 1 meter, which is approximately as big as a 4 year-old!

It was over two cars long!

To defend itself, it would charge forward, lowering its heard just like a rhinoceros. Mind those horns!

This giant plant-eaters' favorite meals were Cycas, fern and other plants that it cut off with its powerful parrot-like **beak**.

Its large bone **collar** protected its neck and shoulders from its enemies and their bites and claws!

To protect their young ones, they would form a **circle** around them. Then they would point their spikes towards their enemy.

In order to become the chief of the herd and attract females, male triceratops had to fight each other, charging into each other, **horns** first!

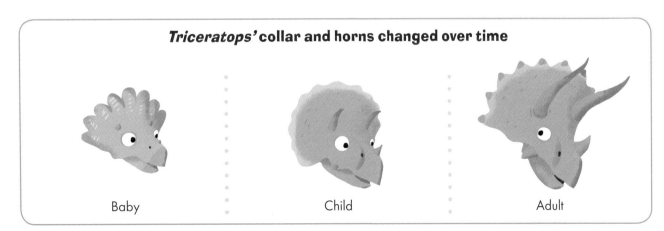

Triceratops' collar and horns changed over time

Baby   Child   Adult

ANKYLOSAURUS

Ankylosaurus was a real war tank. Its bone plates stuck out of its skin, which is where it got its name, meaning "stiff lizard". It also had spikes running along its shoulders, back and tail.

This armored dinosaur lived in the wetlands of North America. It lived towards the end of the Cretaceous period.

It was the biggest and one of the last dinosaurs of its kind.

It fed from plants it could find at ground level.

Its meals included fern, flowers, and other easy-to-cut plants.

A War Tank of a Body

A large fused bone club at the tip of its long tail.

Bone spikes along the length of its back and tail.

Large bone plates covering the top of its body and acting like a shield.

Some smaller plates protecting its skull.

What was this dinosaur's weakness? Its soft belly. If a meat-eater were to flip it on its back, that would be the end of the *Ankylosaurus*.

A pair of triangular-shaped spikes sticking out on each side of its head.

THE CLUB: A VERY EFFICIENT WEAPON

To defend itself, *Ankylosaurus* swiped its tail ...

... from one side to the other ...

... in order to break *T-rex*'s legs!

STEGOSAURUS

With two large rows of diamond-shaped bone plates running along its back, and its tail--featuring four, sharp spikes--*Stegosaurus* was easy to recognize. This unique dinosaur appeared towards the end of Jurassic era in North America.

At sunrise, *Stegosaurus* would stand with its dorsal plates in the sun in order to get warmer.

Then, it would feed on tender leaves and greenery: such as moss, fern and horsetail

It would also eat a few stones to help it digest.

The spikes on its tail could measure up to 1 meter!

As its front legs were shorter than its hind legs, it was nearly impossible for stegosaurus to run.

SOME IMPRESSIVE SPIKES AND PLATES

Stegosaurus' plates were impressive looking ...

... but too thin to protect it from an **Allosaurus** attack.

Luckily, its **spikes** were a wickedly effective weapon.

With a simple swipe of the **tail**, it could pierce the thighs of its meat-eating enemy!

Allosaurus would cry with pain ...

... and leave the scene limping. Not a good day for **Allosaurus**.

A roof on its back!

At first, scientists thought that this dinosaur's plates lay flat on its back, a bit like the tiles of a roof. That's why they named it *Stegosaurus*, which means "roof lizard".

Did you know?

THE END OF THE DINOSAURS

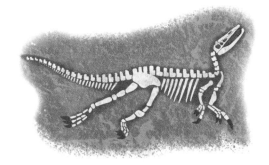

A MYSTERIOUS DEATH

A long time ago, dinosaurs disappeared from the surface of the earth. What happened? It's still a mystery. Scientists have researched several possible reasons. Some are credible. Others seem a bit unbelievable.

ANGRY VOLCANOES

Giant **clouds** of dust may have hidden the sun's rays ...

... turning the entire Earth into **night** for a very long time.

Volcanoes spit fire and let out burning **cinders** and lethal gases ...

... poisoning the air and starting **forest fires** everywhere.

Did you know?

Other animals disappeared at the same time as the dinosaurs.

Marine reptiles

Flying reptiles

DEATH FROM THE SKY

A gigantic **meteor** (a block of rock that's fallen from the sky) collides with Earth.

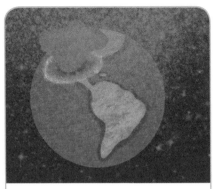

The shock is so violent that it creates a large, heavy **cloud** of black dust ...

... surrounding the earth and **covering** the sun's light for many years.

Without light and heat, **plants** start disappearing ...

... **depriving** plant-eating dinosaurs of food, starving them to death.

Eventually, meat-eating dinosaurs have no prey left to hunt and also **die out**.

OTHER WACKY IDEAS ABOUT THE END OF THE DINOSAURS

Were they poisoned by venomous plants?

Did they die from a contagious disease?

Did male dinosaurs stop being able to mate?

Did mammals eat all of the dinosaur eggs?

Did aliens kill them all?

FINDING FOSSILS

For a very long time, we ignored the existence of the dinosaurs, until the day we found some very strange bones. At first, scientists thought that these giant bones belonged to ... dragons!

Fossils are animal **footprints** or animals and plants remains which were preserved in rock and transformed into stone.

Fossils can be bones, teeth, claws, skeletons, a leaf, an egg, a single footprint or a little poop!

By studying fossils, scientists can understand what dinosaurs looked like and how they lived.

For example, some fossilized poop would contain the remains of the meals they ate and therefore help us to figure out what dinosaurs fed on.

SOME VERY PRECIOUS CLUES
Footprints left in the ground by dinosaurs can tell us many things:

If they walked on two or four legs

If they were small and light or big and heavy

If they lived alone or in herds

And even how fast they could run!

FROM DINOSAUR TO FOSSIL

A **Baryonyx** drowned in the river. First, its flesh would decay and be eaten by fish.

Then, only bones, teeth and claws would be left behind. Little by little, its skeleton gets covered by **sand** and **mud**.

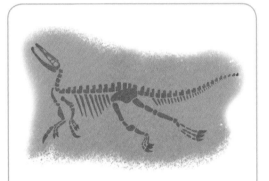

Trapped among a heavy layer of mud, the **skeleton** of the dinosaur is well preserved.

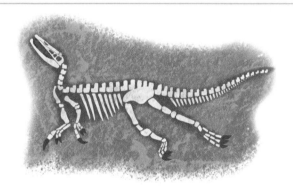

Two million years later, the mud turned into rock and so did the remains of the dinosaur: its skeleton became a **fossil**!

Match the fossil to the dinosaur it belongs to!

Tyrannosaurus Rex – Diplodocus – Triceratops – Therizinosaurus

1

2

3

4

Have fun!

Answers: 1 = *Triceratops*, 2 = *Therizinosaurus*, 3 = *Diplodocus*, 4 = T-Rex

THE RETURN OF THE DINOSAURS

When scientists discover dinosaur remains, it is real detective work! It's a really hard job because bones are often broken and scattered around. Once the fossils are extracted from the ground, they need to be assembled back together--like a jigsaw puzzle.

A Digging Site

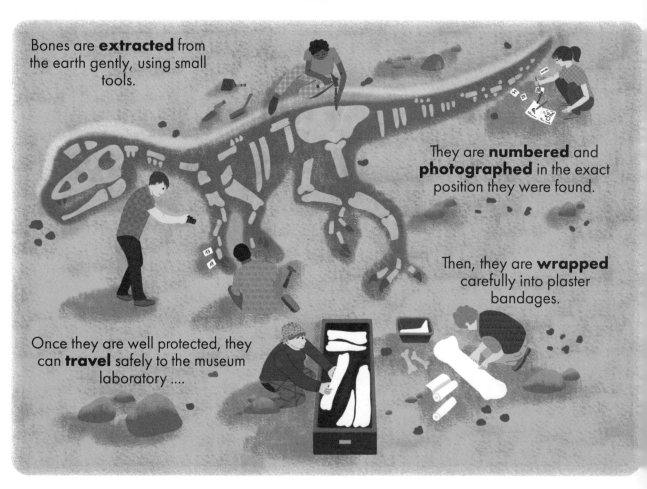

Bones are **extracted** from the earth gently, using small tools.

They are **numbered** and **photographed** in the exact position they were found.

Then, they are **wrapped** carefully into plaster bandages.

Once they are well protected, they can **travel** safely to the museum laboratory ....

...where the scientists will carefully **examen and classify** them. It takes a lot of time!

BRINGING DINOSAURS BACK TO LIFE

The bones are so fragile that scientists have to make special resin molds ...

... that they will use to assemble the pieces of the dinosaur skeleton.

There are so many bones! It's not easy to know where to place them all!

Any missing bones will be recreated.

By taking their inspiration from today's animals, they give dinosaurs muscles ...

... and cover them up with skin.

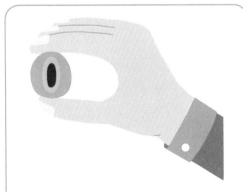

The only thing left to do is to choose a color and add some eyes!

And that's how this beautiful replica of a **Dilophosaurus** was made.

DINOSAURS AROUND THE WORLD

Dinosaur fossils have been found on every continent, including icy Antarctica. Every year, new bones are discovered all over the world!

North America

Ankylosaurus

Plateosaurus

Edmontosaurus

Coelophysis

Triceratops

Pachycephalosaurus

Maiasaura

Diplodocus

Tyrannosaurus

South America

Carnotaurus

Saltasaurus

Eoraptor

Herrerasaurus

Europe

Baryonyx

Polacanthus

Megalosaurus

Pelecanimimus

Carcharodontosaurus

Spinosaurus

Ouranosaurus

Iguanodon

Compsognathus

Olorotitan

Oviraptor

Protoceratops

Tsintaosaurus

Therizinosaurus

Stegosaurus

Fukuiraptor

Asia

Titanosaurus

Africa

Brachiosaurus

Kentrosaurus

Majungasaurus

Lesothosaurus

Australia

Minmi

Savannasaurus

Muttaburrasaurus

Antarctica

yolophosaurus

Glacialisaurus

87

SURVIVORS AND DESCENDANTS

Mysteriously, the catastrophe that killed all dinosaurs, marine and flying reptiles, didn't kill all of the animals. Many species survived, and--most importantly--dinosaurs still have descendants on Earth.

Of the diverse reptile family, crocodiles, turtles, lizards, and snakes survived . . .

... and their descendants, who closely resemble them, still live with us today.

The ancestors of frogs managed to survive, too. Today, their great-great-great ... great-grandchildre are much smaller!

Fish also survived.
The most famous of them: terrifying sharks!

Bugs, spiders and scorpion are still alive today. But thankfully, they are much smaller!

Can you imagine a giant dragonfly flying over your head or a scorpion almost as tall as you? What a nightmare!

THE NEW KINGS OF THE NATURAL WORLD

Mammals thrived with the disappearance of the dinosaurs. They could multiply, grow and occupy more and more land. They became the new kings of the natural world.

lion

brown bear

elephant

gorilla

wolf

squirrel

DINOSAUR "CHILDREN"

It's hard to imagine that the "terrible lizards" could be the ancestors of the sweet parakeet or the cute little robin. However, birds really are the descendants of meat-eating (carnivorous) dinosaurs. In reality, Tweety's distant cousin was a **T-rex**!

Parakeet

Robin

Which of these animals didn't survive the time of the dinosaurs?

1. crocodile **2.** turtle **3.** frog **4.** *Pteranodon* **5.** shark

Have fun!

Answer: 4. *Pteranodon*

INDEX

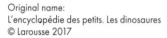

Original name:
L'encyclopédie des petits. Les dinosaures
© Larousse 2017

Original edition produced by:
Edited by Sylvie Bézuel
Publishing Director Sophie Chanourdie,
Editor Marie-Claude Avignon,
Art Director Laurent Carré,
Layout Designer Romuald Gallauziaux,
Manufacturing Rebecca Dubois

Illustrated by
Rebecca Galera (WHAT IS A DINOSAUR?),
Mélisande Luthringer (THE WORLD OF THE DINOSAURS),
Jean-Sébastien Deheeger (LARGE FAMILIES),
Sophie Verhille (LIFE OF THE DINOSAURS, without p. 60-61),
Francois Foyard (DINOSAUR PROFILES, without p. 60-61),
Gaëlle Berthhelet (THE END OF THE DINOSAURS)

CLEVER
•Publishing•

Copyright © Larousse 2017
All rights reserved.

This edition is published under license from
Larousse. For sale in North America only.

First published in the United States in 2019
by "Clever-Media-Group" LLC.

ISBN 978-1-949998-31-3

Contact information for inquiries:
CLEVER PUBLISHING
79 MADISON AVENUE, 8TH FLOOR
NEW YORK, NY 10016
USA
www.clever-publishing.com

10 9 8 7 6 5 4 3 2

MANUFACTURED, PRINTED AND ASSEMBLED IN CHINA